Tree Talk

Tree
Talk

CINDY M. HUTCHINGS

Cindy M Hutch 🌲

featuring black & white photos by
James Rodgers

↑
Hey! That's me!

James Rodgers

MoonPathPress

Cover photo "Sunset After a Day of Rain" by Ronda Broatch
Interior black and white photos by James Rodgers

Book design by Tonya Namura
using Liberation Serifa

MoonPath Press is dedicated to
publishing the best poets of
the U.S. Pacific Northwest

MoonPath Press
PO Box 1808
Kingston, Washington 98346

MoonPathPress@yahoo.com

http://MoonPathPress.com

This collection of poetry is dedicated to my Dad, Duane C.
McMahan, who was the first person to listen to me read these
poems, and to the tall cedar tree that lives across the street
from me...

my poems
profess my love
for you

Acknowledgments

Deep gratitude to the following for showcasing her work:
Washington State Arts Commission (ArtsWA) online
poetry forum *Art with a Heart—Response to Oso* at http://
artwithaheart-forum.tumblr.com, *Quill & Parchment* online
poetry journal at QuillandParchment.com, *Gifts of the Great
Spirit—Volume IV—Legends, Espial 2012, Auburn Reporter*,
and *The New Times*.

Appreciation to Auburn Poet Laureate Marjorie Rommel for all
of her encouragement and support, and to Striped Water Poets
for help generously given in our weekly critique meetings.
Thanks to Lana Hechtman Ayers for her suggestions.

Table of Contents

Tree
Talk

lone tree

dark as forest

beckons

My eyes rest
upon your dark shade

as I rock

unravel my thoughts
into you

unraveling

the cares of this day

waft away

Without care
I see clearly

your steady strength
I reach out

to pluck some
from your branches

Drinking with
Goddess of rain

no one talks much
about Her

but I can see
She quenches

your thirst
like no other

becoming

I drink, quench thirst

with you

Like childhood tree
you bring solace

I can center

when I gaze
upon you

I run constantly

your brethren

feed my breath

When I rest, still
my spinning wheels

you are there, waiting
for my gaze

to fall lightly
upon you

Can I pour my heartache
out to you

Will you take the pain
I feel

deep into your roots
carry my sorrow

through the earth
that beds you

to the killing fields
let them know

I'm sorry

Your higher aspects
I choose to call
my higher power

I pray to you
for my children
reaching for opportunity

gather earth and sky
into a blessing, help them
change their stars

Your neighbors
are getting a trim

better look sharp

preen your
feathered limbs

Mr. Cedar
I'm to write
you every day

I'm fresh out
got no words
there you stand

waiting, expecting
flowery words
worthy of you

It's the shades
of green

from Spring
to midnight

that grace
your bower

confound my eyes
drawing deep

resonant
connectivity

Traveling through
stands of green

I think of your
waiting arms

back home
so far away

I don't lose faith
even though

I love
these others

Returning home
after having strayed

far from your
embrace

being touched
by others

I've found
there are none

who are
your rival

Dark silhouette
against hazy blue sky

falling night
joins your shadow

blurs the lines
you, me

drift along
midnight sea

Dark silhouette
against soft pink sky

falling with
setting sun

tip top bows
in reverence

glories in
engulfing sea

Dark silhouette
against sad gray sky

falling into
sinking gloom

heart seeks
the reservoir

earth's moist flesh
absorbing saline sea

You loom larger
branches accentuated
as night descends

a sentinel
standing guard
over my dreams

how can I
shut the blinds
shutter you

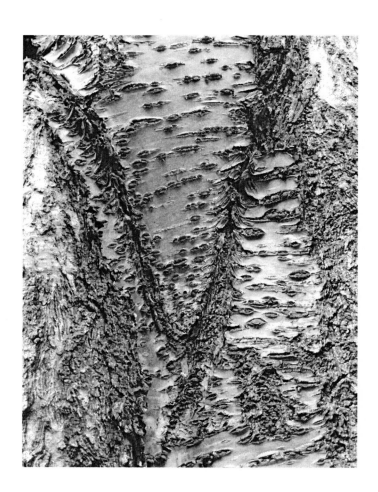

In the Spring
you get lively

with the rising
of your sap

enlivening me

In the Fall
you get quiet

with the waning
of your sap

quieting me

In the Winter
you brace, bend
with the wind

in the Summer
you weather, withstand
all drought

as you
bend, withstand
might I

During one day
under our Washington sky

beautiful morning sun
breeze, wind
gray clouds blow in

misty rain, downpours
dark clouds, lightning
sunbreaks

light plays on grape leaves
white, gray, pink clouds
settling sun

through it all, you
stand unchanging

My challenge
is to learn
to talk to you

but now
the greater task
seems to be

to listen
and hear
you

My thoughts
on you
all day

What will I
say to you?

Do you think
all day
of what you

will say
to me?

Spirit in you

aware
sensual
knowing

in touch with the beings
that live and play
around you

ever blessing all
with your
breath

Might I be
a root

reaching
out from you

in communion
with our mother

Your voice
silent still

breath of air
carries whispers

echoes
in my ears

So easy to forget
to talk with you

get busy, tired
days go by

take for granted
you will always

be here

You wait
to catch

my attention
standing firm

patient
let me know

you're still here

My berry plants
have parched leaves
drying out from no rain

I water their roots
provide moisture

look across the street
at sunlight

playing on, shining through
your lacey green boughs

see the dusty earth
beneath you

hope your caretaker
will give you
a drink

Today, after watering my garden
I glanced over

saw that you
were cut up

your low hanging branches
sawed off, still

lay on the ground
below you

I want to sneak over
gather some

make cedar wands
from your green garlands

that I might keep
a part of you with me

your shorn

beauty

grieves

me

The Stlalacum
fairies that lived

under your canopy

ran for cover
elsewhere

I must now

raise my eyes
to behold

your grace

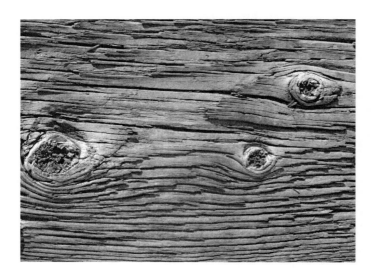

Looking deep
into your eyes

I see your

stubborn strength
fighting hard will

Would that I
be the vine

climbing your sinewy bark
clinging by sweet tendrils

raised aloft by your
grand stature

You stand by
the dark winter
of our keening

the slow night
drags on

you are ever steady

moonlight descends

covers your frosted branchlets

and you shimmer

Avian spirit alights
upon your fringed limb

together waft, sing
a morning song

heralding sun's first rays
breaking through

warming each of you
a moment of reverie

Loved and cared for
by the Universe

not reliant
on man's constructs

you live your life
as you will

About the Author

Cindy Hutchings was born in Seattle, grew up in the Shoreline area, and now lives in Auburn, WA.

She graduated from Green River Community College with an AA degree and High Honors and University of Washington with a BA degree in English and Women Studies, and was initiated into Phi Beta Kappa Society.

She is a member of both Northwest Renaissance and Striped Water Poets. She writes passionately about current events, and local and world-wide social causes. She finds inspiration in the outdoors.

Cindy loves the beach, beach feathers, and beach wish rocks. Her only vice is chocolate.

About the Photographer

James Rodgers started up photography because he didn't like having his photo taken. He has had multiple gallery showings, including being the only male to have shown his work at a Feminist Bookstore in Kent, WA. James has also won many awards for his photography, including prizes through the City of Auburn and a Tacoma Wildlife Refuge. James is also a well-regarded and award winning poet, and recently had a poem and photo published in *Eno Magazine* out of Duke University.